LESSONS TO ~~~~ VE

for Love
OR Nothing

WILLIAM OAK

Guidepost Press ✶ Texas

FOR LOVE OR NOTHING
© 2000 by William Cary Okerlund

All rights reserved. No part of this publication may be
reproduced or transmitted in any form or by any means,
except for the quotation of brief passages in a review,
without prior written permission from the publisher.

Guidepost Press
P.O. Box 690853
Houston, TX 77269

Book design by Sara Patton
Printed in the USA

Library of Congress Catalog Card No. 00-132293

ISBN #0-9678713-0-1

Contents

Introduction 1
1. Empty Pages 7
2. Broken Compass 11
3. The Gold Diggers 17
4. Parable of the Canary 23
5. The Chattering Aspen 33
6. The Well and the Garden 39
7. Parable of the Two Seas 43
8. The Prince's Happy Heart 47
9. Labyrinth 53
10. The Pearl 59
11. The Parable of the Rainbow 65
12. The Bridge Builder 69
13. The Sowing Fields 73
14. Parable of the Pelican and the Whale 77

15.	The Plowman Who Found Content	81
16.	Lion's Hair	89
17.	Most Precious Thing	95
18.	The Burning Bed	101
19.	Parable of the "Tree"	105
20.	The Fishing Pond	109
21.	The Log Fire	113
22.	As Rich as Croesus	117
23.	Parable of the Pink Dolphin	125
24.	For Remembrance	129
25.	A Second Chance	133

I dedicate this book to my wife Diane, who has chosen to come with me on an endless adventure in love.

To my two sons, Nicholas and Cary, who bring out the best of my love.

And most of all to my mother, who taught me all about love in the first place.

If I become a rich man
Yet have not love,
I am nothing.
Only a golden chalice;
Empty without wine.

If I come to be famous
Yet do not have love,
Still, I am nothing.
Only a brilliant star;
Lone without a galaxy.

If I obtain great power,
Yet have not love,
Even still, I am nothing.
Only a mighty fortress;
Over but vast desert land.

Introduction

The more we love, the more we are.

Of all the people in my life, no one better exemplified the truth of these words than my own mother. Somehow it must have been she who one day brought me to conclude that the best in life has to do with people, with what happens between people, and it has a lot to do with love. She loved so many people and so many loved her. Then came the day fate took away her life.

She loved me too, I know. If only I had realized it sooner. Sadly, not until I was twenty, the year she was diagnosed with terminal cancer of the spine and lungs, did I wake up to the knowledge that she dearly cared about me, worried about me when she didn't know my whereabouts (which was often), and that she truly did love me. Before that year, as most children tend to do until they become older, I had not made a conscious effort to get to know her, my own flesh-and-blood mother. The doctors had given her at the most six months to live. I decided then that I would get close to her for the very first time.

It is hard to understand why fate would have it that I didn't wake up to the reality of her love for me until she was diagnosed with cancer. Yet now I look back and see that I was much to blame. I had a chance to get closer to her earlier but was too caught up in my own self-important world. She was always there in my life. From the day I was born, she never stopped loving me, not once. I just didn't take the time to notice. If I could get a message to those others who don't yet realize how much their parents care for them, I would tell them not to make the same mistake I did, not to wait until it is all but too late. And if I could live my life over again, I would become closer to my mother years sooner and would return some of the enormous amount of love she gave me.

Although her death was tragic, I know without a doubt she died happy that she was able to live a good and full life. She lived as life is supposed to be lived. She loved many. She had so much love in her heart. She gave much of it to the seven of us children, much of it to my father, and much to the patients at the home for the aged where she worked for the last thirty years of her life.

Introduction

Many years have since passed, but when I remember my mother, I see her as a living testimony to the miracle of love. Her example has helped me to conclude that the significance of one's life is measured by the depth of one's love for others. For, as one loves more, one's life is given more meaning.

It was this truth that compelled me to write a book about love. When I began to contemplate the task, I soon realized that we are all infants at love. There is so much we need to learn that an entire life-span is barely enough time to do it. Sadly, so many of us haven't gone far beyond the simple acknowledgment that love makes us feel good, and are unable to discover and utilize our full capacity to love. We easily forget that loving someone is a learned ability, a consciously developed skill that requires a great amount of continual hard work.

The other major realization I came to when I began to write this book is that love is many different things. The meaning of love and its mysterious nature elude capture. For this reason, I have compiled twenty-five short allegorical stories, or "lessons" if you will, each of which illustrates an important element of loving relationships. Also interspersed throughout the book are a string of quotations about love designed to illuminate some of its most fundamental tenets. Together, the stories and quotes within this compilation attempt to relay the profound wonder of the phenomenon we call love in such a way that we can begin to apply it to our own relationships of love.

As each of us begins to unfold its riches, we can never let ourselves believe for a moment that we have released into our lives all of love's immense potential. We must never stop learning about love, nor cease nurturing its growth in our lives. For each one of us has a choice between two roads in our lives. One road leads to genuine love, whatever we may ultimately define it to be; the other, to the absence of genuine love. We must realize from the onset that at stake in this choice is the survival of the very meaning and purpose of life.

The absolute value of love makes life worthwhile, and so makes our strange and difficult situation acceptable.

– Arnold J. Toynbee

We are not the same persons this year as last; nor are those we love. It is a happy chance if we, changing, continue to love a changed person.

– W. Somerset Maugham

Empty Pages

One evening a young woman went alone to walk barefoot by the ocean after the sun had set. She stopped in her path and turned so she could see the footsteps she had left in the sand. But they had already been washed away by the waves. When she turned to continue her walk, she was startled by the presence of an old woman wrapped in a blanket who, out of nowhere, appeared sitting by a fire, slowly paging through the leaves of a leather-covered book.

She walked up to the woman and asked, "Where did you come from? I didn't see you here a moment ago. And how did you start this fire so quickly?"

Her questions went unanswered but were instead met with a reply in a serene voice. "Sit with me, child. I have something to show you."

As the young woman sat down beside the fire, the mysterious stranger handed her the book. She curiously turned the pages one by one and was amazed to discover they contained the story of her whole life from the early days of childhood to the present. She then came to the page telling of her encounter with the old woman by the fire during her walk on the beach, but upon turning to the next page, she found it empty. She frantically began to turn the rest of the pages in the book, only to find that they too were all empty. In bewilderment, she looked to the old woman and pleaded with her to explain.

"Does this mean my life ends this night?"

"No, my child. It means tonight your life begins."

At that moment the old woman took the book into her own hands and began to tear out each of the pages with words, throwing them one by one into the fire until all that was left were blank pages.

She handed the book of empty pages to the young woman.

"You see," she said, "just as the waves washed away your footsteps in the sand, your past is forever gone, never to return. The only moment you ever truly possess is here and now. Each new moment is the beginning of the rest of your life and is to be lived to the fullest, for you will not have a chance to live that moment a second time. Most important of all, each new day brings an opportunity to love — one that may never come to you again.

"As for your future, you are free to shape it as you wish, for it has not yet been written."

Then, as mysteriously as she had appeared, the old woman stood to walk away and disappeared into the darkness of the night.

Our love defines a central part of who we are. Our growth in love, an essential part of who we are becoming.

Within oneself is both love's strongest ally and most formidable enemy.

Broken Compass

Early one morning, a young man climbed out of bed, walked sleepily into his bathroom, and stood in front of his mirror. His girlfriend had fallen asleep at his apartment and was still in bed sleeping. They had been dating three years to the day. He knew she had made special plans to celebrate their anniversary. He, on the other hand, had decided the time had come to break up.

Although they still cared deeply for each other, something was missing. He didn't know exactly what it was. All he knew was that the magic was gone and they had fallen into a rut, a rut so deep he wanted out of the relationship.

Still half asleep, he joked with his image in the mirror.

"If only you could become all-knowing for a moment, you could tell me what's gone wrong and show me how to put our love back on track."

He closed his eyes and threw water on his face to wake up. When he wiped his face dry and reopened his eyes, he was startled to see his image in the mirror had taken on a life of its own and was smiling at him. He was even more shocked when his image began to speak.

"You want to know what your problem is? I'll tell you exactly what your problem is. You're steering with a broken compass! Your predicament is much like the story of the captain lost at sea who couldn't find his bearings because he was unknowingly using a compass that had stopped working. All he had to do to get back on track was fix his compass and return on course.

"As for you, breaking up may be the easy way out, but it is surely not the solution. Your girlfriend loves you and you still love her. That's all that really counts. Do you think a good captain would abandon ship because of a faulty compass? Of course not! He fixes his compass and continues sailing. You must do the same. Follow the love in your heart. It will show you the way. Let your heart be your compass and you will soon find things back on track."

The man thought he was losing his mind. He opened the cold-water faucet and closed his eyes again. In rapid-fire progression he splashed a half dozen handfuls of icy water on his face, shook his head briskly, and covered his face with a towel. He was afraid to remove the towel from his face and look at the mirror again. When he finally peeked with one eye at the mirror, he was relieved to see his normal self looking over the edge of the towel.

Still in bed, his girlfriend called to him.

"Sweetheart, did I hear you talking? Is everything all right?"

The man went back into the bedroom and sat down on the bed.

"You wouldn't believe what just happened to me," he said.

Then he realized that she would think he was crazy if he told her, and instead said, "I must have been sleepwalking. I walked into the bathroom still dreaming. It was really strange…"

She replied, "You look like you just saw a ghost. Are you okay?"

"I'm fine," he murmured. "I just need to fix my compass."

"What did you say?" she asked.

For Love or Nothing

"Oh . . . nothing, honey. It has to do with my dream."

He crawled into bed with his girlfriend, told her he loved her, gave her a giant hug, and then softly whispered in her ear, "Happy anniversary!"

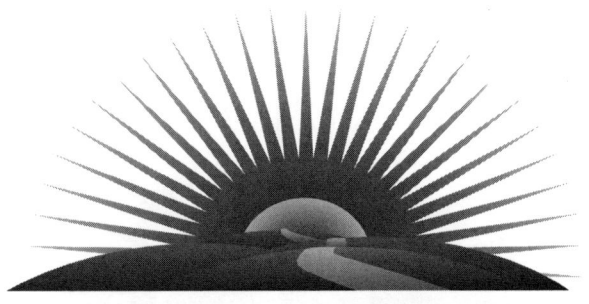

Love is akin to a child learning to walk, who stumbles and falls a thousand times before learning to one day run without fear.

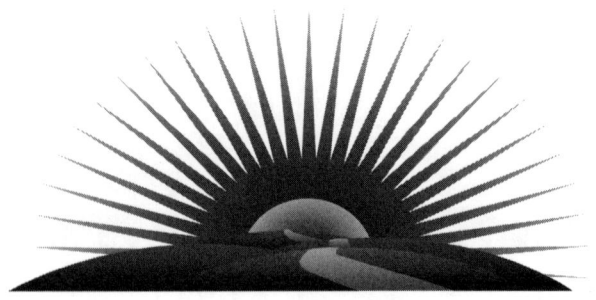

True love is like ghosts,
which everyone talks about
and few have seen.

– La Rochefoucauld

The Gold Diggers

During the days of the Gold Rush, two young friends set out west together with high hopes of striking it rich. They had heard of a small booming town where many were said to have discovered large deposits of gold — the precious metal that made dreams come true.

As they approached the town, they saw the surrounding hills and the nearby river swarming with hundreds of men like themselves. But only a lucky few were still finding gold, and very small chunks at that, for most of the gold in the area had already been thoroughly prospected.

When they arrived, they stopped at the only saloon in town and over a glass of whiskey exchanged talk of what each would do with their riches if they struck gold. In the middle of their conversation the younger of the two friends became so excited he decided he could not wait a minute longer. He jumped off his barstool and urged his friend to accompany him to the hills before losing another second.

But the older man said, "You go join the rest. I'll wait here."

He wished his younger friend luck. Then he ordered another glass of whiskey.

After his friend left, the man pulled up a chair next to one of the old-timers in the saloon, and with a close ear, listened to the long story of how gold was first discovered in the town.

Now, many days passed, but still the older of the two men refused to go out into the hills with his companion and the other men. Instead, he stayed in the saloon day after day talking with all of the old gold diggers passing through town. He asked them many questions about prospecting for gold. Particularly, he asked them how one might go about discovering a cache of gold in a place in the mountain rocks where no one else had ever been before.

His younger friend came back at dusk every day empty-handed but with a head still full of dreams. Each day at dawn, the younger man begged his friend to join him in the hills. But still, each time he replied

The Gold Diggers

without explanation that he would rather remain back at the saloon.

At the end of one day, when his younger friend arrived from the hills with a crowd of other men, he stood up off his barstool to greet them as they entered through the saloon's swinging doors.

"Tomorrow I shall leave town," he said. "I have learned many things about prospecting for gold from the old-timers I have met here. My dream is to find gold in my own way. To discover gold where no man has yet ever been."

He turned to his companion and asked, "Will you go with me?"

The younger man replied, "But there is gold here. Hundreds have already gone home rich. I just need to get lucky enough to find a chunk or two of what's left. Go if you wish, but I'm going to stay."

So the two friends departed, the younger remaining, the older leaving for new territory. But they promised to meet again in the saloon one year from that day to exchange stories of luck and fortune.

Exactly one year later to the day, the two men returned to the saloon as both had agreed. Each of them

For Love or Nothing

had a small pocketsack chock-full of gold-colored nuggets.

The older of the two told his story first. He said with the knowledge he gained from the old-timers, he had struck gold on the side of a distant mountain where no one else had ever been before.

The younger of the two said he hadn't gone anywhere, but had stayed right in town the whole year. He explained to his friend how he had just spent the last of his money to pay another man for the secret to a nearby place few knew about, where there was still an abundance of gold.

With gleams in their eyes, they both poured out the contents of their cloth pocketsacks onto a table. The crowd of men in the saloon gathered to watch. Immediately, all could see that the two piles of nuggets were of a slightly different golden color.

The older of the two men said to his companion, "I can see, my friend, that in all your time searching for the gold of your dreams you have learned very little. You haven't even discovered what true gold is. I'm afraid to tell you that you have just spent the last of your money on nothing but the worthless gold of fools.

"And do you not know that one cannot buy another man's secret to make one's own dreams come true?"

Saddened, the younger man turned without a word and, with a bewildered look on his face, walked out of the saloon to ponder the words of his friend in solitude.

The richest (and truest) love
is that which submits to
the arbitration of time.

– Lawrence Durrell

There is hardly any enterprise which is started with such tremendous hopes and expectations, and yet which fails so regularly as love.

– Erich Fromm

Parable of the Canary

Carlita watched the other newborn canaries fly one by one from the nest until she found herself alone. But she was in no hurry to leave. Unlike the other young canaries, she was terrified of flying.

Quivering with fear, she climbed up to the edge of the nest. Perched on the edge with eyes closed, she waited for a gentle breeze to take her away. When she finally gathered the courage to open her wings, a fierce gust of wind swept her frail body out into the air, tossed her in circles, and sent her crashing to the ground. After she painfully landed head first, another gust of wind took her rolling along the grass. In the tumble, she injured one of her wings.

Raveled, but still in one piece, she decided that if she was going to survive, she had to learn to fly. Though her wing was still sore from the injury, she managed to fly a few feet each try. But that was all. So she hopped, one jumping flutter of about a dozen feet at a time, but nothing more.

She decided to explore the land to find a safe place to live with food nearby. On the foothills of a mountain she found a grassy field each morning abundant with worms. Close by was a farm with a birdhouse filled fresh every day with delicious seed.

It's not a bad life, she thought to herself. But she didn't learn to truly fly. She only hopped slowly from place to place as she needed. Since hopping seemed to suffice, she convinced herself, Why learn to fly when I can easily survive without taking to the sky?

Late one night, however, an old white owl appeared on a tree above and gave Carlita a warning.

"Listen to me, Carlita. You were born to fly and fly you must. Find the Power to Fly. Only when you find it will you be able to fly."

Then the owl flew away into the night sky.

The next morning when she awoke, Carlita remembered the words of the white owl and immediately began her search for the Power to Fly. But the owl didn't tell her where she could find this wondrous power that would give her the ability to fly. So she began asking other feathered creatures that crossed her path.

Parable of the Canary

She came upon a condor who had just come down from the mountains. She asked of the condor, "Do you know where I may find the Power to Fly?"

The condor answered, "I have spent all of my life flying over magnificent high mountains. I have flown higher than any other bird has flown. Each time I rest at the peak of a new mountain, I feel closer to the power of flight. I have been told to find the Power to Fly one must fly to the Top of the World. Far away in a distant land I have seen a mountain higher than any on earth. If you wish, I shall take you there. We can fly to the Top of the World together."

So Carlita agreed and traveled with the condor, clenched to his back. After many weeks of flying they finally came within sight of the great mountain of which the condor had spoken. After a tiring, day-long ascent, they finally arrived at its peak high above the clouds.

Carlita hopped up to the highest point she could find. When she looked around, she saw the most beautiful view she had ever seen in her life. She turned to the condor and said, "Never in my life have I seen anything more magnificent than what you have shown me here atop this mountain. But where, may I ask, is the Power to Fly?"

The condor replied, "I don't wish to disappoint you, but I have not the answer to your question. If you wait here, I'll have a look around."

But the condor didn't return.

After waiting several hours, Carlita realized that what she was searching for was not at the top of the mountain. Without the condor to carry her down, she opened her wings and bravely jumped off the peak to glide slowly down the side of the mountain, often tumbling into the rocks, until she finally arrived at the bottom of the mountain where lay a great ocean.

She came upon a seagull who had just returned from a nearby island.

Carlita asked the seagull, "Do you know where I may find the Power to Fly?"

The seagull answered, "I have spent my life flying to the most beautiful islands of the ocean. At the end of the earth where the ocean begins it is said there is an island more heavenly perfect than any creature can imagine. There, one may live in ecstasy, as food is forever abundant and the climate is always kind. The Power to Fly may be found on the Island of Paradise. I shall take you there."

Parable of the Canary

So they departed over the water, the seagull holding Carlita gently underneath with his feet. They flew for days before they came upon the first small group of islands.

"We still have a great distance to travel," the seagull said.

They continued flying for many days more, then weeks more, slowly, from one chain of islands to the next. Then, after a long stretch of nothing but ocean as far as the eye could see, they came upon a large island all by itself, and landed.

Carlita saw that the island was indeed beautiful and unlike anything else she had ever seen before.

She turned to the seagull. "Never have I seen a place so wonderful as my eyes have seen today. Truly, it is just as heavenly as you described it would be. But please show me where on this island we may find the Power to Fly."

The seagull answered, "I did not bring you all this way to disappoint you, but I'm afraid I don't have the answer to your question. If you can wait here for a while, I'll take a look around."

The seagull left, but when he didn't return, a deep

sadness overtook Carlita. She said to herself, I'll never find the Power to Fly. Maybe it doesn't even exist!

So she found a large piece of driftwood. Clinging to the driftwood, she floated away from the island. After drifting in the ocean for nearly a month, Carlita one day awakened to find herself on the shore of a vast desert plainsland. There, she came upon a hawk who had just descended from the sky.

Carlita asked the hawk, "Perhaps you know where one can find the Power to Fly?"

The hawk replied, "I have spent my days flying closer to the sun than has any other bird. The sun, giver of warmth, light, and life, I have been told, is the source of the power of flight. You must go to the Place the Sun Sleeps. There, it is never cold. There, the sun never stops shining. It is there that you may find the Power to Fly and end your search. If you so wish, we shall together go to the Place where the Sun Sleeps."

Hesitantly, she agreed and the next morning they flew, Carlita clenched to the back of the hawk, directly towards the sun heading due east. By midday they were flying straight upwards into the sun. By dusk they changed course to due west in the direction of the setting sun and continued westward until morning came.

Parable of the Canary

They were very high after the first day, so high that they could not be seen from the ground. They continued the futile eastward, upward, and westward pattern for days, thinking it would become warmer as they got closer to the sun. Instead, it became colder each day that passed.

An entire week went by, and one bitterly freezing day the hawk stopped and said to Carlita, "I don't want to disappoint you, but it appears we aren't getting any closer to the sun. Winter is near and I must leave you to fly south. I won't make it to the warm country if I have to carry you there. I'm sorry—"

"Please stop," Carlita said, "you need not explain. Just go, please. Just leave me alone."

So the hawk left Carlita there, alone up in the sky in the middle of nowhere.

Carlita began to glide slowly downward. She was cold, her wings began to freeze, and she feared she was going to die. Far before she neared the earth, she tired, fainted, and went unconscious.

Again, the mysterious white owl appeared to her in a dream.

"Carlita, wake up!" he said, "You are falling to the earth and are about to hit ground!"

For Love or Nothing

Just before she was about to reach the surface of the earth, she regained consciousness, spread her fragile wings to reduce velocity, and luckily landed in a haystack. When she climbed out and shook the hay off her wings, she was surprised to find the old white owl perched on a fence right next to her.

"Carlita my dear," he said, "many will say they can lead you to what you are searching for, only to take you down a fruitless path. You need not follow anyone but yourself. Nor do you need to go far to find what you are seeking; for it is not hidden in a distant place. I must go now, but leave you with these final words:

> "Know where your search begins,
> For what you seek is found within."

To love nothing is not to live;
to love feebly is to languish
rather than live.

– Fenelon

Love is like a butterfly that when chased eludes capture, but when you look the other way lands quietly on your shoulder.

– Anonymous

The Chattering Aspen

Listen! Do you hear the rustle, rustle of the leaves of that tree over our heads? They are never still. They whisper and chatter all of the time, even when there isn't wind enough to stir a leaf on one of the other trees.

The Indians told a story about the first aspen tree. Come sit nearer, and I will tell it to you.

Years and years ago there was a lake somewhere called Spirit Lake, where the sun always shone and the winds were always soft. Indian spirits lived there, and they were wonderful to look upon. They gleamed as though the never-failing sunshine of their lake glowed within them. They wore golden tunics and mantles, and the feathers in their headbands and on their arrows were tipped with glimmering gold.

But, although they were so splendid and radiant, one of them, whose name was Wahontas, longed for a human bride. Leaving Spirit Lake, he wandered through many Indian camps, looking for the most perfect maiden.

At one tent he found two lovely sisters, Mistosis and Omemee. Mistosis had eyes that gleamed like stars. Omemee had hair that shone like corn.

Wahontas went to their father, the old chief, and asked for the hand of one of his daughters in marriage. The old chief was happy to have such a suitor for his girls. But which one, he asked, did Wahontas wish to marry?

Wahontas pondered the question. They were equally beautiful, but which was the one for him? Then a plan came to him.

He disguised himself as an old, old Indian. Over his gold tunic he threw a ragged cloak, and upon his feet he placed worn moccasins, full of holes. Then he went to the sisters' tent, and found them sitting outside.

A torrent of abuse greeted him as he approached.

"Away! Go away! There is no room for you here!" shouted Mistosis. "Hurry, hurry, we have no time for strange beggars!"

"But I am aged, weary, and hungry," Wahontas said.

The Chattering Aspen

"Aged!" scolded Mistosis. "There should be no aged people in the world. We should not have to take care of them!" On and on went her tongue, scolding, scorning, gibing at the poor old man.

Then Omemee stepped forward. She said no word, but led the old man inside the tent to a seat upon a soft deerskin. Quickly she lit a fire and upon it she cooked her best venison and broth. As he ate she looked sadly at his torn shoes and, going to a corner, brought out her most beautiful moccasins, beaded with blue and gold. She put them on his feet, smiling sweetly at him as she did so, while all the time the tongue of Mistosis went on with its cruel scolding.

In broken words Wahontas thanked Omemee and, tottering to the flap of the tent, he lifted it slowly. Then, in the golden light of the entrance, he paused and drew himself up to his full height. From his shoulders he tore the ragged cloak, from his head he pulled the long white hair that had covered his raven locks.

"I came to you as an old man, weary, hungry, and forlorn," he said. "I come again, not as a beggar, but as a suitor. I have made my choice. Only one of you is beautiful within. Will you have me, Omemee?

"No one should be forced to bear the ceaseless

cruelty of Mistosis' tongue again," he went on. "She shall become the aspen tree, whose leaves are never silent."

As he spoke, Mistosis, amazed and furious, became rooted to the spot. Her arms changed to branches, her tongue to many chattering leaves!

Wahontas turned to Omemee and opened his arms. "Come, my bride, my dove," he said. "Come with me to the golden Spirit Lake, where no cloud of sorrow or pain shall ever dim thy sweet life!"

For a moment Omemee rested in his arms. Then in the form of two doves they flew over the forests to the golden lake, where they dwelled blissfully for years and years. Perhaps they are there today, while in our forests and along our roadsides the leaves of the aspen tree still chatter, chatter, without ceasing!

– Native-American Folktale

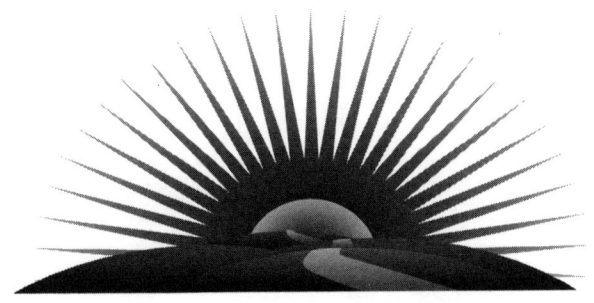

Many a man in love with a dimple makes the mistake of marrying the whole girl.

– Stephen Leacock

The porcupine, whom one must handle gloved, may be respected, but is never loved.

– Arthur Guiterman

The Well and the Garden

He lacked enough food. She needed more water. The irony was they had both recently moved right next to one another into cottages deep in the forest and he had a well on his land while she had a large garden. With the aid of a pump, running water could be delivered to his cottage whenever he needed it. Though he had plentiful water, the only food he had to live on came from hunting the scarce wildlife in the forest and fishing occasionally in a small nearby lake. He wasn't very good at either and suffered horribly for it.

She, on the other hand, laboriously made numerous trips on foot each day to the lake to get the fresh water she needed for herself and her garden. She always had plenty to eat, but the never-ending work to get water completely exhausted her by the end of each day.

The man had longed for a secluded life. On his arrival he had built a wooden fence between the two properties. She found the fence offensive and had planted a row of tall bushes to block the fence from view. The woman didn't want to get involved with anyone either. She purposely avoided conversation on the rare times the two made eye contact. The fence obstructed the view to the other's cottage and because of it neither knew of the other's predicament.

Both enjoyed swimming in the lake, but they carefully adhered to separate routines to avoid crossing paths. After laboring in the garden all day, the woman preferred swimming after dusk so she could avoid being seen. He, on the other hand, made a routine of swimming at the crack of dawn before he started the work of the day so he could watch the sun make its glorious golden appearance over the water.

One day it so happened that the man fell asleep in his boat after fishing all afternoon without a single bite. While he slept, the boat drifted onto shore. He only woke up after nightfall when the woman dove into the lake next to him, unaware of his presence. The boat rocked when he sat up, and the woman saw him. His first impulse was to apologize and get on his way, but instead he explained what happened and started their first conversation.

The Well and the Garden

It didn't take long before both began to talk about their predicaments. When they discovered each other's need, they both naturally offered to help the other. Several days later, he tore down his fence and used the planks to begin construction of a small irrigation ditch from his well to her garden. Knowing he hadn't eaten a good meal for days, she invited him to her cottage that night for a lavish dinner.

She then invited him for a moonlight swim in the lake after dinner. Night after night they dined and swam together, enjoying each other's company increasingly as time passed. Then, one evening at the lake they passionately kissed under the light of the moon to consummate the marriage of their special gifts to one another, of which the well and the garden were only the beginning.

Love is all we have, the only way that we can help each other.

– Euripides, 408 BC

Know that the human heart is a bottomless receptacle for love and holds limitless capacity to produce love, and so be empowered.

Parable of the Two Seas

A very long time ago the Great Maker created two magnificent seas on the land. The Maker was careful to create each of the seas equally, both with abundant fish and fowl for play, crowned by surrounding forests, and both accompanied by two rivers: one arriving every day with fresh water from distant mountains to the north and the other an outlet stretching out to a faraway ocean to the south.

One day the Great Maker decided to bring the two seas to life, so that they could be free to form as each so wished.

Now the first sea said to his Maker, "I do not wish to change in any way from what I am today.

"The two rivers you have blessed me with have become dear companions to me. New water from the mountains replenishes my depths constantly and my overflow has an outlet to the ocean. What more could I

For Love or Nothing

wish for? I am encompassed by glorious forests and have become accustomed to the many swimming and feathered creatures who have found a home in me. I cannot improve what you, the Great Maker, have already created as perfectly as anyone could wish."

Now the other sea, once alive and free to form as he pleased, thought much differently than the first.

"I am tired of these bothersome waters perpetually arriving from the mountains and never allowing me to rest," said the second sea to himself.

So with rocks, boulders, and mud, he blocked up the mouth of the northern river arriving from the mountains, and the river had to find a more friendly sea nearby into which it could flow.

Soon after he had blocked the river from the north, the sea saw that the southern river was slowly taking large parts of his body out to the ocean. He became angry and rushed to also block up the mouth of the river to the south with more rocks, boulders, and mounds of earthen clay to halt the outward flow.

When the sea was finished he said to himself, "Now I may finally rest in peace without the nuisance of those two troublesome rivers."

Parable of the Two Seas

As the years passed, the water of the sea became stagnant from being without replenishment or outlet. The fish in the sea eventually perished, the birds had to find another home, and over time the forest land surrounding the sea turned to desert.

The sea then realized with sorrow what he had done to himself. But he could not turn back the clock. And for the rest of the life of the sea, he is reminded of his error so fatal by each passerby that says, looking onto the lifeless body of water, "There lies the Dead Sea," as they wonder how it became that way.

The great tragedy of life
is not that men perish,
but that they cease to love.

– W. Somerset Maugham

As selfishness and complaint
pervert and cloud the mind,
so love with its joy clears
and sharpens the vision.

– Helen Keller

The Prince's Happy Heart

Once upon a time there was a little Prince in a country far away from here. He was one of the happiest little princes who ever lived. All day long he laughed and sang and played. His voice was as sweet as music. His footsteps brought joy wherever he went. Everyone thought this was due to magic. Hung about the Prince's neck on a gold chain was a wonderful heart. It was made of gold and set with precious stones.

The godmother of the little Prince had given the heart to him when he was very small. She had said as she slipped it over his curly head: "To wear this happy heart will keep the Prince happy always. Be careful that he does not lose it."

All the people who took care of the little Prince were careful to see that the chain of the happy heart was clasped. But one day they found the little Prince in his garden, very sad and sorrowful. His face was wrinkled into an ugly frown.

For Love or Nothing

"Look!" he said, and he pointed to his neck. Then they saw what had happened.

The happy heart was gone. No one could find it, and each day the little Prince grew more sorrowful. At last they missed him. He had gone, by himself, to look for the lost happy heart that he needed so much.

The little Prince searched all day. He looked in the city streets and along the country roads. He looked in the shops and in the doors of the houses where rich people lived. Nowhere could he find the heart that he had lost. At last it was almost night. He was tired and hungry. He had never before walked so far or felt so unhappy.

Just as the sun was setting the little Prince came to a tiny house. It was very poor and weather-stained and stood on the edge of the forest. But a bright light streamed from the window. So he lifted the latch, as a Prince may, and went inside.

There was a mother rocking a baby to sleep. The father was reading a story out loud. The little daughter was setting the table for supper. A boy of the Prince's own age was tending the fire. The mother's dress was old. There were to be only porridge and potatoes for supper. The fire was very small. But the family was as

The Prince's Happy Heart

happy as the little Prince wanted to be. Such smiling faces and light feet the children had. How sweet the mother's voice was!

"Won't you have supper with us?" they begged. They did not seem to notice the Prince's ugly frown.

"Where are your happy hearts?" he asked them.

"We don't know what you mean," the boy and the girl said.

"Why," the Prince said, "to laugh and be as happy as you are, one has to wear a gold chain about one's neck. Where are yours?"

Oh, how the children laughed! "We don't need to wear gold hearts," they said. "We all love each other so much, and we imagine that this house is a castle and that we have turkey and ice cream for supper. After supper Mother will tell us stories. That is all we need to make us happy."

"I will stay with you for supper," the little Prince said.

So he had supper in the tiny house that was a castle. And he played that the porridge and potato were turkey and ice cream. He helped to wash the dishes,

For Love or Nothing

and then they all sat about the fire. They imagined that the small fire was a great one, and they listened to fairy stories that the mother told. All at once the little Prince began to smile. His laugh was just as merry as it used to be. His voice was again as sweet as music.

He had a pleasant time, and then the boy walked part of the way home with him. When they were almost to the palace gates, the Prince said: "It's very strange, but I feel just exactly as if I had found my happy heart."

The boy laughed. "Why, you have," he said. "Only now you're wearing it inside."

– Author Unknown

Fail to first love yourself,
and your love for others
will surely fail.

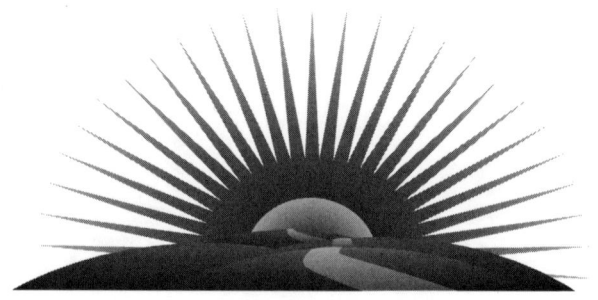

The way to love anything is to realize it might be lost.

– G.K. Chesterton

Labyrinth

One night, when a newlywed couple were sound asleep in their bed, the husband dreamt he was visited by a genie who told him, "I will grant you any wish your heart desires."

The man was deeply in love with his wife, and without hesitation he said, "I have only one wish. To live for a hundred years and have my loving wife still at my side."

The genie replied, "Your wish may surely be granted. But before I can grant you a wish such as this, you and your beloved must first pass a test. Let me forewarn you before you accept the challenge of my test, if you should fail, I am afraid you may instead find yourself a man in lonely solitude long before your life ends."

"For this wish to come true," the man said, "my beloved and I will pass any test you can devise."

For Love or Nothing

So the genie woke the man's sleeping wife and took both of them far away to a strange land where stood a large garden labyrinth. She explained to the young couple that the labyrinth contained countless passages and for the man's wish to come true, they must choose the correct path that would lead them out on the other side together.

The man protested that such a test was too difficult.

The genie said, "There is a simple secret in choosing the right passageway each time, which I cannot reveal. But rest assured, it is easier than it appears."

"So be it," the man agreed. "We will pass your silly test!"

The genie left the two alone to enter the labyrinth. As soon as they did, they immediately came to a choice between two different passageways. In trying to decide which way to go, they began to argue. The woman felt compelled to continue through the passageway on the right, but the man wanted to go through the passageway on the left. After what soon turned into a mildly heated exchange of words, the man finally conceded and they continued through the right-hand passageway.

Labyrinth

But soon they found themselves in the same dilemma. The man again felt certain the passageway on the left was correct and she felt it was the one on the right. This time, after another long argument, the man's wife conceded to his chosen path.

They continued on, passageway after passageway. Sometimes they picked the same path but most of the time they differed and argued until one of them finally gave in to the other. Both were near exhaustion when they entered a large open area with two wide passageways from which they again had to choose. As had happened many times before, each stubbornly insisted on different directions. This time neither could find the will to concede. The man felt they were nearing the other side and was convinced that he was right. Likewise, the woman was certain she was right.

After a long time arguing without nearing agreement, the man decided he would alone try the passageway of his choice and leave his wife behind, hoping to return to her later with news of discovering the way out of the labyrinth. As soon as he entered the passageway, he found himself having to choose between two new directions which he did quickly now that he was alone. Then he began to run through the labyrinth, randomly choosing directions until, all of the sudden, he found himself on the outside.

Elated to have found the way out, the man re-entered the labyrinth but soon became confused and lost. He ran through the maze of passageways for endless hours but was unable to find the way back to his beloved wife. He hopelessly fell to the ground and cried for the genie to return.

The genie reappeared and spoke to him. "Your beloved did not wait for you to return. She, too, continued through the passageway of her choice. She also found her way out. The secret I did not tell is that all of the paths in the labyrinth eventually lead out to the other side. The real test was only to see if you two would stay together until the end. This test you have failed. I am afraid to say that long before your life ends you may find yourself a lonely man in solitude."

The man woke from his dream in a panic sweat, frantically swung his arm over his wife, and embraced her with all his strength. She woke up startled and when she asked what was the matter, he muttered, "I had a terrible dream and all I know is the only thing in the whole world that really matters is that we always stay together."

Labyrinth

As she looked at him quizzically, he told her that if he could have any wish he wanted, he would live to be a hundred with her still at his side and not let anything tear them apart.

Love is giving and sometimes giving means giving in.

Trust is the cement
without which
love shatters.

The Pearl

Once upon a time in a small fishing village on the coast of a distant country, a young man and woman met, fell in love, and soon afterwards married. The two had come from different parts of the country. He was born in a village on the southern coast, and she came from a mountain village to the north. As did nearly everyone in the village, they earned their living by harvesting oysters. They both worked hard every day until they were one day able to build a modest house for themselves with the money they made in oyster trade. They lived happily in the new home and enjoyed their simple life together.

Then one day something happened that would change their lives forever. In the harvest of the day the man found a unique oyster that was much larger than any he had ever seen before. He revealed his find with excitement to his wife. They decided they wouldn't sell the oyster but would instead open it for themselves.

When they pried the oyster halves apart, they discovered a magnificent white pearl inside.

They had found other pearls before in the oysters they had harvested, but this one was larger than a marble and its beauty was more spectacular than any either had seen before. Its smooth lustrous surface was so beautiful they chose not to sell it, but instead to keep it as a secret treasure between them.

The two made a solemn vow to each other that no other hand except their own would ever be allowed to touch the wonderful pearl. No other villager or person would be allowed even to lay eyes on the pearl and, of course, they could tell absolutely no one of its existence. They put the pearl in a cloth and kept it in a dresser drawer in their bedroom under lock and key. Every night before they went to bed they brought out the pearl to hold in their hands, to touch its smooth white surface and behold its beauty. Before they put the pearl away, they together repeated the same words each night in confirmation of their vow: "This pearl is ours and only ours. That is what makes it forever special."

Seven years passed. All of this time they kept their oath to each other and the beautiful pearl remained their secret treasure.

The Pearl

One day, however, the man was tempted when his wife went away for a few days to visit the place of her birth. While she was gone, another woman from the village stopped by his door one night to offer her company over a glass of wine. He saw no harm in her overture and allowed the woman to come into his home. After finishing her bottle of wine, he brought out a bottle of his own, which they also finished. The two became happily drunk and talked into the late hours of the night.

Then he made the mistake he would live to regret his entire life. He told the woman about the pearl. Though he insisted he couldn't show it to her, she begged and seduced him until he couldn't say no. Before he brought it out into the open, he made her promise she would not touch it. But upon seeing the pearl's magnificence, she snapped it out of his hands before he could stop her.

Realizing what he had done, the poor man began to cry. She returned the pearl and left him to weep alone. When he looked at the pearl in the morning, he saw that it had lost some of its luster. Though almost unnoticeable, it had become slightly tainted with a yellowish color.

For Love or Nothing

He hoped his wife wouldn't see the difference. But when she returned and they looked at the pearl in the candlelight before going to bed as they had done many times before, she immediately saw that the pearl had changed. She pretended as if she didn't notice the change and said nothing to him. Before they put the pearl away, they repeated the words they had said together a thousand times before. But the words had lost their meaning.

That evening as they laid in bed facing apart with eyes open wide all night long, the woman began to wonder what had happened. She knew her husband must have allowed someone else to touch and hold the pearl. She convinced herself that it was another woman. As she laid in bed unable to sleep, she decided in her fury that she would get even with him the first chance she had.

Such an opportunity came some months later when her husband had sailed more than a day's journey down the coast to harvest oysters. While he was away, she invited a young man from the village into her home. Without remorse or hesitation, she revealed the pearl to the man and placed it in his hands. But he was not impressed by its beauty, for the moment he

The Pearl

touched it, all of its luster was suddenly lost. It was no longer white, but had turned a ghastly taint of yellow.

After the young man left, the once magnificent pearl continued to change appearance until it eventually turned dull black in color, its beauty gone forever. When the husband returned and saw the pearl, he immediately knew what had happened. From that day forward their love would never be the same, for they trusted each other no more. They kept the blackened pearl only to remind them of their regrettable mistake.

Lies, always, are poison to love.
It is not wise to play with poison.

Stubbornness creates a battlefield in which two entrenched souls refuse to compromise. Unwilling to surrender ground, the two are slowly pulled into all-out war.

The Parable of the Rainbow

When the Sun and Rain first met, they fought each other in fierce battle, for both wanted to dominate the sky. The Sun declared, "Only I shall rule the sky! My glorious rays give the earth warmth and light."

The Rain retorted, "My nourishing waters give the earth no less than life itself. The earth cannot exist without me. Only I deserve to rule the sky! I will spread out my clouds and not let you pass through."

The Sun replied, "The earth needs me, not you. I will burn your clouds until they dry up and disappear. I will not allow your cold darkness to rule the face of the earth."

The two battled for centuries without decisive victory. Each could gain only temporary control of the skies. The Rain did not have enough clouds to cover the whole face of the earth. Though the Sun was many times successful in drying up the clouds, the Rain never failed to regroup and form new clouds to reblanket the earth.

Only the earth suffered when one held the upper hand. When the Sun dominated, drought destroyed the land. When the Rain ruled, floods drowned nearly all the life that was left after the Sun's deadly heat.

When they realized they were slowly destroying what they both loved most, the two great forces in nature, the Sun and the Rain, decided to end their old feud. They saw the folly of believing one is more important than the other and acknowledged they each had something equally valuable to give.

So it is that now, whenever these two great forces of nature meet in the same place, instead of warring, they together form a colorful rainbow as a symbol of their truce.

It is good to have many
goals in life as long as one
of them is to love fully.

To build love without friendship is to construct a pyramid upside down.

Without a strong foundation, it tumbles as one tries to build.

The Bridge Builder

There was once a man who lived in a house on the bank of a river. One day he decided he would build a small bridge that would take him across the river, where lived a girl he dearly loved. The man had never before built a bridge. He had seen many other bridges from a distance and saw no need to make a design before he began. So, without a clear plan, he started to build.

He first built a bridge of bamboo and rope attached to the trees on both sides of the river. But it didn't last. Eventually terrible winds came and tore the ropes from the trees. The bamboo structure floated down the river.

He built a second bridge of cedar planks on a few cedar pilings pounded into the river bed. But it didn't last either. The awesome force of the river's steady currents eventually tore the cedar pilings loose. Again, the whole structure floated down the river.

For Love or Nothing

Finally, he said to himself, "If I am to build a bridge to my beloved that will last, I must use stronger materials. I must use more pilings and drive them deeper into the river bed if they are to withstand the strength of the river's turbulent currents. It would also be wise to draw a clear design to follow so I won't fail again."

In his mind, he visualized a perfect bridge, sturdy and strong, made of oak planks on many strategically spaced solid oak pilings. He then made a small drawing of his new design. Even before he began to build, he knew with absolute certainty that this bridge to his beloved would surely be strong enough to last a lifetime.

Friendship is a single soul, dwelling in two bodies.

– Aristotle, 322 BC

While the heart is busy building bridges, beware, the ego will be busy building barriers.

Some go through life
letting love happen, but it
is better to go through life
making love happen.

The Sowing Fields

Once there lived two couples who had each moved from the city and bought farm houses side by side out in the country. Their first year in the countryside, both couples decided to grow enough food in their fields to live off the land. Early their first spring, they set out to plant crops for the season, but each couple took a different approach to cultivation.

The first couple tilled their soil beforehand to prepare the ground for seeding. Then, together they planted their seeds with great care. With irrigated water from a ditch they had laboriously dug out together during the winter before, they moistened the newly planted seeds until they sprouted.

Throughout the summer the husband gently plowed in between the rows of crops day in and day out to remove the never-ending growth of weeds. Each and every day the wife routed water throughout the field to assure that all of the crop received moisture during the summer's frequent dry periods. At the end of summer, they rested. Their months of hard toil could be seen in callused palms and sun-bronzed faces.

Now the second couple approached the cultivation of their field with a much simpler technique. They didn't tend to their crop daily as did the first. Rather, they decided to plant their seeds and simply let nature take its course. They convinced themselves that their crop would grow without labor. All they did was pray for rain.

In early fall the two couples went out to harvest their fields. They each gathered their crops. Each of them canned and stored all they had grown during the summer. But only one couple had grown enough to last through winter.

One must sow love, if one is to reap love. But only by daily cultivation will the harvest be abundant.

We must resemble each other
a little in order to understand
each other, but we must be a
little different to love each other.

– Paul Geraldy

Parable of the Pelican and the Whale

One bright day a pelican was flying over the ocean when he spotted the back of a monstrous blue whale in the distance. The pelican had never before seen a whale, so he decided to fly closer to take a look. Just when he arrived a few feet overhead, the whale spouted a powerful geyser of sea water that directly hit the unsuspecting pelican and sent him on an unwelcome wet ride forty feet into the air.

The pelican shouted down to the whale, "Hey! Watch what you're doing!"

The whale replied, "Next time, stay out of the way!"

After their turbulent first words, the two continued to talk. The pelican had many questions to ask the whale.

"How can you breathe under the water? Are you not cold all of the time down there? It must be terrible to

For Love or Nothing

live in the shivering depths of the ocean! Worst of all, from where you live, you can't see land, can you? How could anyone ever live in the sea! You poor creature."

The whale said, "I would surely not like to live in the sky as you. What a terrifying way to live, with nothing beneath you except air. You must constantly work to avoid a fall. Rest for one short second and down you go! What a horrible way to live!

"As for me, it is a wonderful and easy life I have. I can rest whenever I want. The sea is a beautiful place to live, with fish of every color, reefs of intricate design, and the sparkle of the sun's rays."

"But you have no idea what you're missing down there," the pelican said. "If you could see things through my eyes, you would understand how glorious life can be in the sky. I wish we could change places for a day. Then you could see how beautiful my world really is."

"And if you could see life though my eyes," the whale said, "you would see how good life is under the sea as well."

As soon as they said these words, the two creatures began to change in appearance. Their wish was becoming true. When the transformation was complete, they each found themselves in the other's body.

Parable of the Pelican and the Whale

The whale found himself in the body of the pelican flying in midair. Terrified to death, he immediately landed on the water. The pelican was equally frightened when he, all of the sudden, found himself inside the body of the whale. It took both of them a while to get used to the different way of life, but when they did, they began to explore the wondrous new worlds each had just entered.

The transformation lasted for a whole day. The two creatures were both happy to return to their own bodies, but since that day neither spoke a single bad word about each other's world. They had learned a lesson they would cherish in their memories all of their lives.

Respect is love in plain clothes.
– Frank Byre

Love alone is capable of uniting living beings in such a way as to complete and fulfill them, for it alone takes them and joins them by what is deepest in themselves.

– Pierre Teilhard de Chardin

The Plowman Who Found Content

A plowman paused in his work one day to rest. As he sat on the handle of his plow he began to contemplate. The world had not been going well with him as of late, and he could not help feeling downhearted. Just then he saw an old woman looking at him over the hedge.

"Good morning!" she said. "If you are wise you will take my advice."

"And what is your advice?" he asked.

"Leave your plow, and walk straight north for two days. At the end of that time you will find yourself in the middle of a forest, and in front of you there will be a tree towering high above the others. Cut it down, and your fortune will be made."

With these words the old woman hobbled down the road, leaving the plowman wondering. He unharnessed

For Love or Nothing

his horses, drove them home, said good-bye to his wife, and then, taking his ax, started out.

At the end of two days he came to the tree, and set to work to cut it down. As it crashed to the ground a nest containing two eggs fell from its topmost branches. The shells of the eggs were smashed, and out of one came a young eagle, while from the other rolled a small gold ring.

The eagle rapidly became larger and larger, until it was of full size. Then, flapping its wings, it flew up.

"I thank you, honest man, for giving me my freedom," it called out. "In token of my gratitude take the ring—it is a wishing ring. If you wish anything as you turn it around on your finger, your wish will be fulfilled. But remember this—the ring contains but one wish, so think well before you use it."

The man put the ring on his finger, and set off on his homeward journey. Night was coming on when he entered a town. Almost the first person he saw was a goldsmith standing at the door of his shop. So he went up to him, and asked him what the ring was worth.

The goldsmith looked at it carefully, and handed it back to the man with a smile.

The Plowman Who Found Content

"It is of very little value," he said.

The plowman laughed.

"Ah, Mr. Goldsmith," he cried, "you have made a mistake this time. My ring is worth more than all you have in your shop. It's a wishing-ring, and will give me anything I care to wish for."

The goldsmith felt annoyed and asked to see it again.

"Well, my good man," he said, "never mind about the ring. I dare say you are far from home, and are in want of some supper and a bed for the night. Come in and spend the night in my house."

The man gladly accepted the offer, and was soon sound asleep. In the middle of the night the goldsmith took the ring from his finger, and put another just like it in its place without disturbing the plowman in the least.

The next morning the countryman went on his way, not knowing of the trick that had been played on him. When he had gone, the goldsmith closed the shutters of his shop and bolted the door. Then, turning the ring on his finger, he said, "I wish for a hundred thousand sovereigns!"

For Love or Nothing

Scarcely had the sound of his voice died away than there fell about him a shower of hard, bright, golden sovereigns. They struck him on the head, on the shoulders, on the hands. They covered the floor. Presently the floor gave way beneath the weight, and the goldsmith and his gold fell into the cellar beneath.

The next morning, when the goldsmith did not open the shop as usual, the neighbors forced open the door, and found him buried beneath the pile.

Meanwhile the countryman reached his home, and told his wife of the ring.

"Now, good wife," he said, "here is the ring; our fortune is made. Of course we must consider the matter well. Then, when we have made up our minds as to what is best, we can express some very big wish as I turn the ring on my finger."

"Suppose," the woman said, "we were to wish for a nice farm. The land we have now is so small as to be almost useless."

"Yes," the husband said, "but on the other hand, if we work hard and spend little for a year or two we might be able to buy as much as we want. Then we could get something else with the wishing-ring."

So it was agreed. For a year the man and his wife

The Plowman Who Found Content

worked hard. Harvest came, and the crops were splendid. At the end of the year they were able to buy a nice farm, and they still had some money left.

"There," he said. "We have the land, and we still have our wish."

"Well," his wife said, "we could do very well with a horse and a cow."

"They are not worth wishing for," he said. "We can get them as we got the land."

So they went on working steadily and spending wisely for another year. At the end of that time they bought both a horse and a cow. The husband and wife were greatly pleased with their good fortune, for, said they, "We have got the things we wanted and we have still our wish."

As time went on everything prospered with the worthy couple. They worked hard, and were happy.

"Let us work while we are young," they told each other. "Life is still before us, and who can say how badly we may need our wish someday?"

So the years passed away. Every season saw the bounds of the farm increase and the granaries grow fuller. All day long the farmer was about in the fields,

For Love or Nothing

while his wife looked after the dairy. Sometimes, as they sat alone in the evening, they would remember the unused wishing-ring, and would talk of things they would like to have for the house. But they always said that there was still plenty of time for that. And they smiled at each other, and were content.

The man and his wife grew old and gray. Then came a day when they both died—and the wishing-ring had not been used. It was still on the man's finger as he had worn it for forty years. One of his sons was going to take it off, but the oldest said, "Do not disturb it. There has been some secret in connection with it. Perhaps our mother gave it to him, for I have often seen her look longingly at it."

Thus the old man was buried with the ring, which was supposed to be a wishing-ring, but which, as we know, was not, though it brought the old couple more good fortune and happiness than all the wishing in the world could ever have given them.

– Retold by Julia Darrow Cowles

Life has taught us that love
does not consist of gazing
at each other but in looking
outward in the same direction.

– Saint-Exupery

Love is the child of illusion
and the parent of disillusion.

– Miguel de Unamuno

Lion's Hair

In a village in the mountains of Ethiopia, a young man and a young woman fell in love and became husband and wife. For a short while they were perfectly happy, but then trouble entered their house. They began to find fault with each other over little things — he blamed her for spending too much at the market, or she criticized him for always being late. It seemed not a day passed without some kind of quarrel about money or friends or household chores. Sometimes they grew so angry they shouted at each other, and yelled bitter curses, and then went to bed without speaking, but that only made things worse.

After a few months, when she thought she could stand it no longer, the young wife went to a wise old judge to ask for a divorce.

"Why?" asked the old man. "You've been married barely a year. Don't you love your husband?"

"Yes, we love each other. But it's just not working out."

"What do you mean, not working out?"

"We fight a lot. He does things that bother me. He leaves his clothes lying around the house. He drops his toenails on the floor. He stays out too late. When I want to do one thing, he wants to do another. We just can't live together."

"I see," said the old man. "Perhaps I can help you. I know of a magic medicine that will make the two of you get along much better. If I give it to you, will you put aside these thoughts of divorce?"

"Yes!" cried the woman. "Give it to me."

"Wait," replied the judge. "To make the medicine, I must have a single hair from the tail of a fierce lion that lives down by the river. You must bring it to me."

"But how can I get such a hair?" the woman cried. "The lion will surely kill me."

"There I cannot help you." The old man shook his head. "I know much about making medicines, but I know little of lions. You must discover a way yourself. Can you do it?"

Lion's Hair

The young wife thought long and hard. She loved her husband very much. The magic medicine might save their marriage. She resolved to get the hair, no matter what.

The very next morning she walked down to the river, hid behind some rocks, and waited. After a while, the lion came by to drink. When she saw his huge claws, she froze with fear. When he bared his sharp fangs, she nearly fainted. And when he gave his mighty roar, she turned and ran home.

But the next morning she came back, this time carrying a sack of fresh meat. She set the food on the ground two hundred yards from the lion, and then hid behind the rocks while the lion ate.

The next day she set the meat down one hundred yards away from the lion. And on the following morning, she put the food only fifty yards away and stood nearby while he gulped it down.

And so every day she drew closer and closer to the fierce, wild beast. After a while she stood near enough to throw him the food, and finally came the day when she fed him right from her hand! She trembled as she watched the great teeth ripping and tearing the meat. But she loved her husband more than she feared the

For Love or Nothing

lion. Closing her eyes, she reached out and pulled a single hair from the tail.

She ran as fast as she could to the wise old judge.

"Look!" she cried. "I've brought a hair from the lion!"

The old man took the hair and looked at it closely.

"This is a brave thing you have done," he said. "It took a great deal of patience and resolve."

"Yes," said the woman. "Now give me the medicine to make my marriage better!"

The old man shook his head.

"I have nothing else to give you."

"But you promised!" the young wife cried.

"Don't you see?" asked the old man gently. "I have already given you all the medicine you need. You were determined to do whatever it took, however long it took, to gain a magic remedy for your problems. But there is no magic remedy. There is only your determination. You say you and your husband love each other. If you both give your marriage the same patience and resolve and courage you showed in getting this hair, you will be happy together for a long time. Think about it."

And so the woman went home with new resolutions.

– An Ethiopian Folktale

All things of value come at a price. If one wants love, one has to work for it.

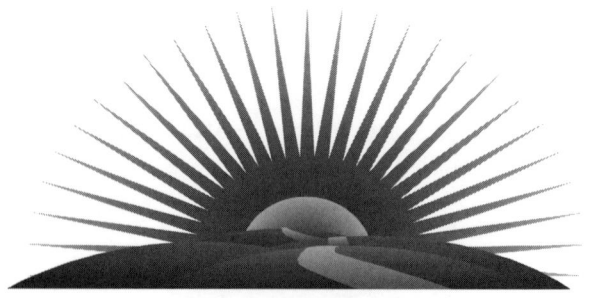

For love to endure, one must attach supreme value to one's growth in love.

Most Precious Thing

It happened long ago that a young man and a young woman fell in love with each other and decided to marry. They had almost no money, but they did not hesitate over that. Their trust in each other gave them faith that their future together must be a bright one, as long as they had each other. They happily chose a date on which they would join hearts and souls.

Before the wedding, the girl came to her fiancé with a request. "I cannot imagine our ever wanting to be apart," she said. "But it may be, in time, we will tire of each other, or that you will be angry with me, and want to send me back to my parents' house. Promise me that if this should happen, you will allow me to carry back with me the thing that has grown most precious to me."

Her fiancé laughed, and could see no sense in what she asked, but the girl was not satisfied until he had written down his promise and signed his name to it. Then the two were married and began their life together.

They set their minds to improving their worldly position. They were both willing to work hard at it, and soon their patient industry found reward. Their first successes made them even more determined to put poverty behind them, and they worked harder than ever before. Time passed, and their purses swelled. They became comfortable, then well-to-do, and finally rich. They moved to a bigger house, found a new set of friends, and surrounded themselves with all the trappings of fortune.

But in their single-minded pursuit of wealth, they began to think more of their things than of each other. More and more, they quarreled about what to buy, or how much to spend, or how they should go about increasing their riches.

One afternoon, as they were preparing a feast for several important friends, they argued about some trifling matter—the flavor of the gravy, or perhaps the order of seating at the table. They began shouting and accusing each other.

"You care nothing for me!" the husband cried. "You

think only of yourself, and the jewels and fine clothes you wear. Take those that are most precious to you, as I promised, and go back to your parents' house. There is no point in our staying together."

His wife went suddenly pale, and stared at him with a distracted look in her eyes, as if she had just seen something for the first time.

"Very well," she said quietly. "I am willing to go. But we must stay together one more night, and sit side by side at our table, for the sake of appearances in front of our friends."

The evening arrived. The feast began. It was as bountiful as their ample means allowed. When, one by one, the guests had succumbed to its influence, and her husband too had fallen asleep, the good woman had him carried to her parents' cottage and laid in bed there.

When he woke the next morning, he could not understand where he was. He raised himself up on his elbow to look about him, and at once his wife came to the bedside.

"My dear husband," she said softly, "your promise was that if you sent me away I might carry with me the most precious thing. I care for you more than anything else, and nothing but death shall part us."

For Love or Nothing

At once the man saw how selfishly they had both acted. He clasped his wife in his arms, and they kissed each other tenderly. That same day they returned home and began to devote themselves once again to each other.

– Folktale from Eastern Europe

Love is that condition
in which the happiness
of your beloved becomes
essential to your own.

– Robert A. Heinlein

The love we give away
is the only love we keep.

– Elbert Hubbard

Love built on beauty,
soon as beauty, dies.

– John Donne

The Burning Bed

A very beautiful woman lived by a lake on the outskirts of a small town. Ever since she was a little girl, people everywhere had told her she was very pretty. She heard it so often she naturally had become a bit conceited. When she was a teenager her shapely figure aroused the attention of many young men who dated her and poured unceasing flattery upon her. Strikingly attractive as an adult, she had become so caught up with herself that she habitually admired her image in a mirror every chance she had, from the moment she awoke to the moment she fell asleep.

When her handsome lover told her how especially ravishing she looked when her face and body were softly lit by the glow of candlelight, the words went to her head. She began a bedtime ritual of lighting a myriad of candles on her bedstand to admire herself in a small hand-held mirror before blowing out the candles and falling asleep in contemplation of her beauty.

For Love or Nothing

Her lover often told her that it was her beauty within that he loved most. He reminded her that one day her skin would become wrinkled and her face would age, but he would still love her because the beauty within the heart never fades away. Too consumed with herself, she didn't hear these words. She refused to imagine a time she would lose her youth.

One night, she fell asleep in her robe with all of the candles lit. A gust of wind from an opened window knocked the candles over and onto the bed. When she awoke to the horror, the bed was already engulfed in flames. Her robe on fire, she ran out of the house and threw herself into the lake to quench the flames...but not before her face and body had become severely burned.

The next morning her lover found her lying on the shore of the lake unconscious and he rushed her to the hospital. Weeks later when she returned home, she looked at herself in the mirror and cried when she saw the ghastly figure she had become. Her lover comforted her, reminding her what he had always told her: that it was her beauty within he loved and that this beauty deep within her heart would never fade away. He loved her until the hair on her head turned gray.

Love looks not with the eyes, but with the mind; and therefore is a winged Cupid painted blind.

– Shakespeare

Love should be a tree whose roots are deep in the earth, but whose branches extend to heaven.

Parable of the "Tree"

From the top floor of the campus library a young man saw in the distance a single colorful and towering tree on the shore of the bay. The autumn tree stood out strikingly from the others around it. Dressed in orange and red, its upper limbs stretched far above the tree line in the horizon. A lover of trees, he decided to go down to the shore to see this one more intimately.

When he arrived at the shore, he was surprised to discover this "tree" was in fact really two giant redwoods. As one stood directly behind the other, they appeared to be one from a distance. Although one tree looked to be older, as it was much wider than the other, both trees had massive trunks, and both reached over a hundred and fifty feet into the sky. He reckoned the two majestic redwoods must have been there for at least a hundred years before he was even born.

He was so intensely fascinated with the trees he began to carry on a conversation with them. In his imagination, they became two living creatures and he had many questions to ask.

"You must be very best friends to have lived so long together?"

The older of the two was first to speak. "Let the truth be known we had a very troubled beginning. You see I was here first, being born some twenty years before her. When she first sprouted only a half a dozen yards away, I issued a firm warning. I told her there wasn't enough room for us both. My roots had already grown nearly under her feet and I was not about to share the ground with someone else!

"The strong-willed one she is, she paid no heed to me and quickly spread her roots as deep as she could, though I tried to choke her off from the earth around her. I even tried to block the sun from her limbs to stunt her growth, but all to no avail. For she was determined to catch up to my height. Soon enough she did just that. Before I knew it, she was full grown and we shared the top of the tree line together."

She then added her part of the story. "It was at that time I became as feisty as ever. I wanted to prove he couldn't bully me around. We wrestled in the wind, constantly fighting over sunlight. We both paid dearly

Parable of the "Tree"

and lost many branches during our fiercest battles. In dry times we fought over the water under our feet.

"Then one day after we had both grown to be over a hundred years old, we decided to make peace. We made a covenant that day. I surrendered the sky in front of me, and he gave me the sky behind him. It is for this reason one side of us remains nearly empty, but together we are complete. In dry times we shared the ground's water evenly between us. Our roots have since grown intertwined together.

"It is a much better way to live. We still wrestle in the wind at times, but our quarrels never last more than a moment. Although in truth we stand separately, we are seen as one tree from a distance. In fact, we have learned to grow as one so much, in a very special way we have truly become one."

The young man woke from the trance his imagination had placed on him. He said to himself, what a beautiful story if it were true.

The course of love never did run smooth.
– Shakespeare

If you want to be loved,
be lovable.

– Ovid

The Fishing Pond

A young couple lived in a small house near a large pond plentiful with trout. Every few days one of them would take their turn to go out to the pond to fish. Since the trout was the mainstay of their diet they were always careful not to take too many fish and to return small catch so the trout could replenish. As long as they did this, the pond continued to give them all the food they needed to eat.

One year, however, it became apparent that the fish weren't as plentiful as they had been over the years. When this meant their meals couldn't be as hearty as they had become accustomed to, they both began to keep every fish they caught. Secretly they each cooked and ate the small catch alone before returning home. This went on for several months.

The stock of the pond began to slowly diminish

For Love or Nothing

until the day it was nearly impossible to catch any trout at all. Finally the two confessed what they each had been doing and they promised never to do it again. After many years the pond was eventually replenished with fish.

Know not to do to your beloved what you would not want them to do to you.

– Anonymous

Love is, above all,
the gift of oneself.

– Jean Anouilh

Love dies only when growth stops.

– Pearl S. Buck

The Log Fire

After seven years of marriage, love had lost its flame. Both husband and wife admitted the passion they once knew had long disappeared. They decided to spend two weeks alone in a log cabin in the mountains to rekindle the fire gone dormant.

They arrived in the middle of a winter as bitterly cold as their marriage had become. The only heat in the cabin was provided by a fireplace that had to be fed by logs. It quickly became the center of their time together. The two sat in front of the fireplace for hours at a time just to stay warm. Covered with a thick layer of blankets, they fell asleep many times cuddled on the rug in front of the fireplace.

They took turns feeding the fireplace with logs to keep it burning at all times, for without the fire's warmth the icy air outside quickly penetrated the cabin walls. They also took turns waking up early in the freezing morning hours to restart the fire that never

For Love or Nothing

failed to die out in the middle of the night. They spent nearly all their time rediscovering love either in bed under the covers, or romantically in front of the fireplace... talking all day and late into the night in each other's arms.

After a few days the fire became neglected at times. One day they lost track of whose turn was next and the whole day passed with neither attending to the log fire. Both waited to see if the other would take up the task, but neither did. Only when their fire had burned down to mere embers and the cabin had become deathly cold did one of them at last add logs to prevent the fire from going out completely.

It was then that an analogy of the flame with their marriage became abundantly clear to them both. They realized that all one needs to do to keep love alive is remember to feed the fire.

Love works only
as long as we do.

The supreme happiness
of life is the conviction
that we are loved.

– Victor Hugo

As Rich as Croesus

Some thousands of years ago there lived in Asia a king whose name was Croesus. The country over which he ruled was not large, but its people were prosperous and famed for their wealth. Croesus himself was said to be the richest man in the world, and so well known was his name that, to this day, it is not uncommon to say of a very wealthy person that he is "as rich as Croesus."

King Croesus had everything that could make him happy—lands and houses and slaves, fine clothing to wear, and many beautiful possessions. He could not think of anything that he needed to make him more comfortable or contented.

"I am the happiest man in the world," he said to himself.

It happened one summer that a great man from across the sea was traveling in Asia. The name of this

For Love or Nothing

man was Solon, and he was the lawmaker of Athens in Greece. He was noted for his wisdom and, centuries after his death, the highest praise that could be given to a learned man was to say, "He is as wise as Solon."

Solon had heard of Croesus, and so one day he visited him in his beautiful palace. Croesus was now happier and prouder than ever before, for the wisest man in the world was his guest. He led Solon through his palace and showed him the grand rooms, the fine carpets, the soft couches, the rich furniture, the pictures, the books. Then he invited him out to see his gardens, orchards, and stables, and he showed him thousands of rare and beautiful things that he had collected from all parts of the world.

In the evening as the wisest and richest men of the world were dining together, the king said to his guest, "Tell me now, O Solon, who do you think is the happiest of all men?" He expected that Solon would say, "Croesus."

The wise man was silent for a moment, and then he said, "I have in mind a poor man who lived in Athens and whose name was Tellus. He, I doubt not, was the happiest of all men."

This was not the answer that Croesus wanted, but

he hid his disappointment and asked, "Why do you think so?"

"Because," Solon said, "Tellus was an honest man with a big heart who labored hard for many years for the betterment of his family and to give his children a good education. To watch the children he loved grow up and one day become able to do for themselves gave him great joy. When he was an old man, his children were always close to him and they each in their own way returned the love he had given them. After being blessed with beautiful grandchildren, he died a most happy man. Can you think of anyone who is more deserving of happiness?"

"Perhaps not," answered Croesus, half choking with disappointment. "But who do you think ranks next to Tellus in happiness?" He was quite sure now that Solon would say, "Croesus."

"I have in mind," Solon said, "two poor fishermen I knew in Greece who lived on the Aegean Sea. Every day they went fishing in the sea and came home in the afternoon to their lovely wives and sons. They were best friends and had much in common, for they both loved the sea and they both deeply loved their families with all their heart. One could see by the glow in their eyes that they both lived to the fullest each and every day. When both died about the same time, they were cremated and their remains were tossed together into the sea they loved."

Then Croesus was angry. "Why is it," he asked, "that you make me of no account and think that my wealth and power count for nothing? Why is it that you place these poor working people above the richest man in the world?"

"O King," said Solon, "one cannot say whether one is happy or not until one dies, for no one knows what misfortunes may overtake them. Nor do you know if one day misery may be yours in place of all this splendor. Most important of all, true happiness comes from surrounding yourself with those you love most, your family and friends, not by surrounding yourself with riches."

Many years after this there arose in Asia a powerful king whose name was Cyrus. At the head of a great army he marched from one country to another, overthrowing many a kingdom and attaching it to his great empire of Babylon. King Croesus with all his wealth was not able to stand against this mighty warrior. He resisted as long as he could. Then his city was taken, his beautiful palace was burned, his orchards and gardens were destroyed, his treasures were carried away, and he himself was made prisoner.

"The stubbornness of this man Croesus," said King Cyrus, "has caused us much trouble and the loss of many good soldiers. Take him and make an example of him for other petty kings who may dare to stand in our way."

When the soldiers received this command they seized Croesus and dragged him to the marketplace, handling him roughly all the time. Then they built up a large pile of dry sticks and timber taken from the ruins of his once-beautiful palace. When this was finished they tied the unhappy king in the middle of it, and one of the soldiers ran for a torch to set it on fire.

"Now we shall have a merry blaze," said the savage fellows. "What good can all his wealth do him now?"

As poor Croesus, bruised and bleeding, lay upon the pyre without a friend to soothe his misery, he thought of the words that Solon had spoken to him years before: "One cannot say whether one is happy or not until one dies," and he moaned, "O Solon! O Solon! Solon!"

For Love or Nothing

It so happened that Cyrus was riding by at that very moment and heard his moans. "What does he say? he asked of the soldiers.

"He says, 'Solon, Solon, Solon!'" answered one.

Then the king rode nearer and asked Croesus, "Why do you call on the name of Solon?"

Croesus was silent at first. But after Cyrus repeated his question kindly, he told all about Solon's visit at his palace and what he had said.

The story affected Cyrus deeply. He thought of the words, "No one knows what misfortunes may overtake them." He wondered if sometime he, too, would lose all his power and be helpless in the hands of enemies.

"After all," he said, "ought not men have compassion for those who are in distress? I will do to Croesus as I would have others do to me." And he caused Croesus to be given his freedom, and ever afterwards treated him as one of his most beloved friends.

– Heroditus (retold)

We are each of us angels with only one wing. And we can fly only by embracing each other.

– Luciano de Crescenzo

Learn to give your love away
and forever strong it will stay.

Parable of the Pink Dolphin

Early one morning, a young woman was about to go swimming in the ocean when she saw a pink dolphin stranded on the other end of the beach. She ran to the dolphin lying half-dead on the sand, and gently pulled him back into the ocean. The moment the pink dolphin returned to the water he revived, and began to play affectionately with the young woman who had saved his life. The two swam happily together for hours in the morning sun.

Then the dolphin raised his head out of the water and began to speak. "Thank you for saving my life. For your act of kindness, you may wish for anything your heart desires and it will surely come true."

The young woman thought about it for a little while and then said, "I wish to be happy until the end of my years."

For Love or Nothing

The magical dolphin brought his nose up to the woman's face and whispered into her ear. He then swam away and was never seen again.

As time passed, those who met the woman thought she was indeed the happiest person they had ever known. Whenever someone asked her what was the secret to her happiness, she simply smiled and replied, "I listened to the wise words of a magical pink dolphin whose life I saved."

The woman grew to be very old and eventually became close to death. Her children feared that the words of the pink dolphin might never be known, so they pleaded with their mother moments before she passed away, "Please tell us the secret words of the magical dolphin."

The old woman smiled and spoke her last words:

"He told me to show compassion to everyone I could, for the rewards would return to me doubled."

Love is not only inexhaustible,
it increases with the giving.

Love seeks to make happy
rather than to be happy.

– Ralph Conner

For Remembrance

A man sat by the coffin of the one who had been nearest to him, in black and bitter care. And as he sat, he saw passing beyond the coffin a troop of bright and lovely shapes, with clear eyes and faces full of rosy light.

"Who are you, fair creatures?" asked the man.

And they answered: "We are the words you might have spoken to her."

"Oh, stay with me!" the man cried. "Your sweet looks are a knife in my heart, yet still I would keep you, for she is cold and deaf, and I am alone."

But they answered: "Nay, we cannot stay, for we have no being, but are only a light that never shone."

And they passed on and were gone.

Still the man sat in black and bitter care.

For Love or Nothing

And as he sat he saw rising up between him and the coffin a band of pale and terrible forms, with bloodless lips and hollow eyes of fire.

The man shuddered.

"What are you, dreadful shapes?" he asked.

And they answered: "We are the words she heard from you."

Then the man cried aloud in anguish: "Depart from me, and leave me with my dead! Better solitude than such company."

But they, sitting down in silence, fixed their eyes upon him, and they stayed with him forever.

– Adapted from Laura E. Richards

Love does not cause suffering;
what causes it is the sense of
ownership, which is love's opposite.

– Saint-Exupery

For one human being to love another: that is perhaps the most difficult of all our tasks; the ultimate, the last test and proof, the work for which all other work is but preparation.

– Rainer Maria Rilke

A Second Chance

I'm dead, the man thought. Moments before, his skull had smashed into his windshield during a head-on collision. All that night and just before the accident, he had been thinking about his impending divorce. His wife wanted to try again to works thing out, but he had become so disillusioned about their unhappy marriage, he had given up all hope.

He knew his two girls would suffer horribly because of the decision, but he felt he had little choice. The constant arguments had become so hateful, the damage done to the marriage was irreparable. It was better to live apart and at peace, rather than together in continual battle.

The man was asking himself how a marriage that had begun in euphoria could end up like this when he saw the headlights. A drunkard, asleep at the wheel, veered directly into his path. The next thing he knew, he was floating in the air looking down at his dead body. Blood was streaming down the side of his head. As he watched, a doctor arrived on the scene and declared him dead. He felt warm and very peaceful. So this is what it's like to be dead, he thought. It's beautiful.

Then, all of the sudden, the man felt he was floating through a long tunnel. At the end of the tunnel he saw a radiant being of light standing before him. Beyond the being of light was what appeared to be another realm of existence. Perhaps it is heaven, he thought.

"Wait," the angelic being said. "You are not ready to pass into the afterlife, for you must first learn the lesson of forgiveness."

"Forgiveness?" the man said.

"Yes. Your marriage failed because in all of your life you never learned how to forgive. You must go back and learn to forgive your parents for their abuses when you were a child, and to forgive yourself for your own failings. Only then will you finally be able to forgive your spouse as well. Once you have learned forgiveness, you will be able to love her fully and completely, and will so find happiness in your marriage. Only then will you be ready to pass into the afterworld."

A Second Chance

The next thing he knew, he was back in his body and in terrible pain. As blood rushed over his eyes, he let out several piercing screams. He continued wailing as the doctor returned back to the scene. But he screamed not because of the terrible pain. He cried because he knew that the being of light he had encountered was right. He had never forgiven the very people in his life he cared about the most. Yet, for the first time in his life, he now knew with absolute clarity that this was exactly what he had to do.

Love is an act of endless forgiveness.

– Peter Ustinov

If I have the gift of prophecy; and can fathom all mysteries and possess all knowledge; and have a faith that can move mountains; but have not love, I am nothing.

– I Corinthians 13:2